THE QUAKER OATS
TREASURY OF BEST RECIPES

SMITHMARK

INTRODUCTION

Mention Quaker® Oats and steaming bowls of hot cereal and homemade cookies fresh from the oven immediately come to mind. Quaker oatmeal has been a favorite hot cereal since its introduction over 100 years ago, and most of us have grown up eating Quaker Oats. The popularity of Quaker Oats as a recipe ingredient has also continued to grow ever since recipes were first printed on the box early in the 1890s.

The recipes on the box have changed over the years, but the main ingredient – whole grain oats – has stood the test of time. What makes oats a whole grain? A whole grain is simply what the name implies – a grain that is whole. Nothing has been added to the oats and nothing has been taken away. Because of this, oats provide fiber, vitamins and minerals, have one of the highest levels of protein compared to other grains, and are 100% natural – free of preservatives, artificial ingredients, sugar, sodium and cholesterol.

But Quaker Oats are more than a nutritious breakfast cereal. The versatility of oats makes them a popular ingredient in a variety of convenient, creative and delicious recipes. In *The Quaker Oats Treasury of Best Recipes*, we are proud to present 30 of our all-time favorites. Each taste-tempting recipe in this collection includes step-by-step directions and photographs to make them especially easy, as well as tips to ensure success every time! We hope such tasty selections as Raisin Oatmeal Cookies, Banana Orange Muffin Cake and Italian Stuffed Meat Loaf become your family favorites for years to come.

CLB 2602
©1992 Colour Library Books Ltd, Godalming, Surrey England.
Text ©1992 Quaker Oats Company.
All rights reserved.
This edition published in 1992 by
SMITHMARK Publishers Inc., 112 Madison Avenue, New York, NY 10016
Printed and bound in Singapore.
ISBN 0 8317 3197 4

SMITHMARK books are available for bulk sales promotion and premium use. For details write or telephone the Manager of Special Sales, SMITHMARK Publishers Inc., 112 Madison Avenue, New York, NY 10016. (212) 532-6600.

Contents

Quaker and the Quaker logo are
registered trademarks of the Quaker Oats Company.

GOLDEN GRANOLA WITH MIXED FRUIT

Serves 12

Prepare this tasty granola right in the baking pan!

3½ cups Quaker Oats (quick or old fashioned, uncooked)
⅓ cup (5⅓ tbsps) margarine, melted
⅓ cup honey
¼ cup firmly packed brown sugar
1 tsp vanilla
1 cup chopped mixed dried fruit

STEP 3

1. Heat oven to 350°F.

2. In a 15 x 10-inch baking pan, combine all ingredients except fruit; mix well, spreading evenly.

3. Bake 20-25 minutes or until golden brown, stirring after 10 minutes.

4. Cool completely. Stir in fruit.

STEP 2

Microwave Directions: In large microwaveable bowl, combine all ingredients except fruit. Microwave at HIGH 3 minutes; stir. Microwave at HIGH an additional 3-4 minutes or until golden brown, stirring after 2 minutes. Spread onto foil; cool completely. Stir in fruit.

Cook's Notes

TIME: Preparation takes 10 minutes, baking takes 20-25 minutes.

PREPARATION: Melt margarine in 1 cup glass measure in the microwave at HIGH about 45 seconds. Use same measure for honey so it will not stick.

VARIATION: Substitute raisins for mixed dried fruit.

SERVING IDEA: Pack lunch bags with granola for a nutritious snack. Can serve with milk, yogurt or fresh fruit.

COOK'S TIP: Store tightly covered up to 1 week.

CHOCOLATE LOVER'S OATMEAL

Serves 2

Rich and delicious, this cereal will please the chocolate lovers in your family.

1¼ cups chocolate milk or milk
⅔ cup Quaker Oats (quick or old fashioned, uncooked)
⅛ tsp salt (optional)
1 tbsp semi-sweet chocolate pieces

STEP 2

1. In medium saucepan, bring milk just to a boil.

3. Cook about 1 minute for quick oats or 5 minutes for old fashioned oats, stirring occasionally.

STEP 1

STEP 3

2. Stir in remaining ingredients.

Microwave Directions: For quick oats, combine all ingredients except chocolate pieces in 2-qt. microwaveable bowl. Microwave on HIGH 4-5 minutes. Stir in chocolate pieces; let stand 1 minute.

Cook's Notes

⌊ TIME: Preparation takes 3 minutes, cooking takes 1-5 minutes depending on the type of oats.

? VARIATION: To microwave old fashioned oats, microwave at MEDIUM-HIGH (70% power) 6-7 minutes.

◻ SERVING IDEA: Serve with additional milk, if desired.

TANGY FRUIT AND NUT MUESLI

Serves 6

For a quick and easy breakfast, prepare this fruit-packed cereal ahead of time. Refrigerate and enjoy throughout the week, hot or cold.

3 cups oranges or tangerines (about 3 large)
1¾ cups water
1⅓ cups Quaker Oats (quick or old fashioned, uncooked)
½ cup pitted, chopped dates
½ cup coarsely chopped nuts
½ tsp ground cinnamon

2. Combine all the ingredients; mix well.

STEP 2

1. Peel, seed and chop the oranges.

STEP 1

3. Cover; refrigerate overnight. Serve cold or hot.

STEP 3

Cook's Notes

⌚ TIME: Preparation takes 15 minutes.

◨ PREPARATION: For thicker muesli, drain excess liquid before serving or heating in microwave.

❓ VARIATION: Substitute raisins, figs or apricots for dates.

◯ SERVING IDEA: Serve with milk or yogurt, if desired.

🍳 COOK'S TIP: Store tightly covered in refrigerator up to 1 week.

BANANA AND BERRIES OATMEAL

Serves 2

Start your day off right with this easy-to-make hot cereal.

1 cup water
⅔ cup Quaker Oats (quick or old fashioned, uncooked)
½ cup mashed ripe banana (about 1 medium)
2 tbsps strawberry or red raspberry preserves
¼ tsp salt (optional)

STEP 3

1. In medium saucepan, bring water to a boil.

2. Stir in remaining ingredients.

3. Cook about 1 minute for quick oats or 5 minutes for old fashioned oats, stirring occasionally.

STEP 2

Microwave Directions: For quick oats, combine all ingredients in 2-qt. microwavable bowl. Microwave on HIGH 3-4 minutes; stir. Let stand for 1 minute.

Cook's Notes

⏱ TIME: Preparation takes 5 minutes, cooking takes 1-5 minutes depending on type of oats.

❓ VARIATION: To microwave old fashioned oats, cook at MEDIUM (50% power) 5-6 minutes.

⬜ SERVING IDEAS: Serve with milk, if desired. Drizzle preserves over cooked cereal in decorative fashion instead of stirring into cereal.

BERRY POWER DRINK

Serves 2

Try this icy cold juice shake that's bursting with flavor – it makes a great healthy breakfast or any-time snack.

1 cup cranberry juice
1 cup fresh or frozen strawberries
One 8-ounce carton vanilla low-fat yogurt
⅔ cup Quaker Oats (quick or old fashioned, uncooked)
1 cup ice cubes
Sugar to taste

1. Place all ingredients except ice in blender container.

STEP 1

2. Cover; blend on HIGH speed about 2 minutes or until smooth.

STEP 2

3. Gradually add ice, blending on HIGH speed an additional minute or until smooth. Serve immediately.

STEP 3

Cook's Notes

🕐 TIME: Preparation takes 5 minutes.

◆ PREPARATION: Plenty of ice is the key to the cold, creamy texture of this breakfast drink.

CARROT OATMEAL MUFFINS

Makes 1 dozen

Carrots and raisins team up to create these wholesome, low-fat oatmeal muffins.

Muffins
1⅓ cups all-purpose flour
1 cup Quaker Oats (quick or old fashioned, uncooked)
¾ cup shredded carrots (about 2 medium)
½ cup raisins
½ cup firmly packed brown sugar
1 tbsp baking powder
1 tsp ground cinnamon
½ tsp baking soda
½ cup skim or low-fat milk
2 egg whites, slightly beaten
⅓ cup (5⅓ tbsps) margarine, melted
1 tsp vanilla
Glaze (optional)
½ cup powdered sugar
1 tbsp skim or low-fat milk

1. Heat oven to 375°F.

2. Spray 12 medium muffin cups with no stick cooking spray or line with paper baking cups.

3. For muffins, combine first eight ingredients; mix well.

4. Add combined ½ cup milk, egg whites, margarine and vanilla, mixing just until moistened.

STEP 4

5. Fill prepared muffin cups ¾ full.

STEP 5

6. Bake 25-30 minutes or until golden brown.

7. For glaze, combine ingredients; drizzle over warm muffins. Serve warm.

Cook's Notes

TIME: Preparation takes 15 minutes, baking takes 25-30 minutes.

FREEZING: Wrap securely in foil or place in freezer bag; seal, label and freeze up to 3 months.

APRICOT OAT BREAD

Serves 18

The subtle flavor of tangy apricots and a kiss of orange makes this "quick" bread a delicious, anytime favorite.

1 cup boiling water
1¼ cups Quaker Oats (quick or old fashioned, uncooked)
1 cup firmly packed brown sugar
3 eggs, slightly beaten
½ cup (1 stick) margarine, softened
1¾ cups all-purpose flour
2 tsps baking powder
1 tsp baking soda
1¼ cups chopped dried apricots
1½ tsps grated orange peel

STEP 3

1. Heat oven to 350°F. Grease a 9 x 5-inch loaf pan.

2. Pour water over oats and set aside.

4. Add oats; mix well.

5. Stir in combined flour, baking powder and baking soda.

6. Add apricots and orange peel; mix well. Pour into prepared pan.

7. Bake 60-70 minutes or until wooden pick inserted in center comes out clean. Cool 10 minutes; remove to wire rack. Cool completely.

STEP 2

3. Beat brown sugar, eggs and margarine at medium speed of electric mixer until smooth.

STEP 7

Cook's Notes

TIME: Preparation takes 20 minutes, baking takes 60-70 minutes.

SERVING IDEA: This delicious bread is perfect for breakfast or a snack.

FRUITED OAT SCONES

Makes 1 dozen

These easy-to-prepare scones are perfect for a leisurely brunch or afternoon tea.

1½ cups all-purpose flour
1¼ cups Quaker Oats (quick or old fashioned, uncooked)
¼ cup sugar
1 tbsp baking powder
¼ tsp salt (optional)
⅓ cup (5⅓ tbsps) margarine or butter
One 6-ounce package (1⅓ cups) diced dried mixed fruit
½ cup milk
1 egg, slightly beaten
1 tsp sugar
⅛ tsp cinnamon

---

1. Heat oven to 375°F.

2. Combine first five ingredients; mix well.

3. Cut in margarine until mixture resembles coarse crumbs; stir in fruit.

STEP 3

4. Add milk and egg, mixing just until moistened.

5. Shape dough to form a ball. Turn out onto floured surface; knead gently 6 times.

STEP 5

6. On lightly greased cookie sheet, pat out dough to form 8-inch circle. With sharp knife, score round into 12 wedges; sprinkle with combined sugar and cinnamon.

STEP 6

7. Bake about 30 minutes or until golden brown. Break apart; serve warm.

Cook's Notes

⏱ TIME: Preparation takes 15 minutes, baking takes 30 minutes.

❓ VARIATION: Substitute currants or raisins for mixed fruit.

⭕ SERVING IDEA: Serve with cream cheese, fruit preserves or whipped butter.

PEPPER CHEESESTIX

Makes 2 dozen

Romano cheese teams up with coarsely ground black pepper and fresh-from-the-garden chives to add a spicy touch to these savory stix. They're great served with salads and soups, or alone as a satisfying snack.

1 cup Quaker Oats (quick or old fashioned, uncooked)
1 cup all-purpose flour
⅓ cup grated Romano or Parmesan cheese
1 tbsp baking powder
¾-1 tsp coarsely ground pepper
½ tsp baking soda
2 tbsps chopped chives or 2 tsps freeze-dried chives (optional)
3 tbsps margarine
¾ cup buttermilk
1 egg white, slightly beaten

STEP 5

1. Heat oven to 450°F.

2. Combine first seven ingredients; mix well.

3. Cut in margarine until mixture resembles coarse crumbs.

4. Add buttermilk, mixing just until moistened.

5. Turn out onto lightly floured surface; knead gently 10 times.

6. Pat dough into rectangle about ½-inch thick; cut into 4 x ½-inch strips with sharp knife.

STEP 6

7. Place on an ungreased cookie sheet; brush tops with egg white.

8. Bake 10-12 minutes or until golden brown. Serve warm.

Cook's Notes

⏱ TIME: Preparation takes 15 minutes, baking takes about 10 minutes.

▢ SERVING IDEA: Great with soups or salads or as a snack.

✳ FREEZING: Wrap securely in foil or place in freezer bag; seal, label and freeze up to 3 months.

WHOLEGRAIN SALLY LUNN

Makes one 10-inch round loaf

This easy, rich bread perfectly complements any light meal.

2¾-3 cups all-purpose flour
1 cup Quaker Oats (quick or old fashioned, uncooked)
½ cup sugar
1 package quick-rising active dry yeast
½ tsp salt
½ cup water
½ cup milk
½ cup (1 stick) margarine or butter, melted
3 eggs

1. Grease 10-inch plain or fluted tube pan.

2. Combine 1 cup flour, oats, sugar, yeast and salt.

3. Heat water, milk and margarine until very warm (120°F-130°F).

4. Add milk mixture and eggs to dry ingredients; beat until smooth. Stir in enough remaining flour to make a stiff batter.

5. Cover; let rise in warm place about 40 minutes or until doubled in size.

6. Stir down dough; pour into prepared pan. Cover; let rise about 40 minutes or until doubled in size.

7. Heat oven to 400°F.

STEP 3

STEP 6

8. Bake 25-30 minutes or until golden brown. Cool on wire rack 5 minutes; remove from pan. Serve warm.

Cook's Notes

⏱ TIME: Preparation takes 20 minutes, rising takes 1 hour 20 minutes and baking takes about 30 minutes.

◣ PREPARATION: Check temperature of warm water with an instant read thermometer. Water that is too warm will kill the yeast culture.

◎ SERVING IDEAS: Serve with soup, stew or salad, if desired. Slice and toast for breakfast; serve with cream cheese, jam or preserves.

❗ WATCHPOINT: Keep dough away from drafts while rising.

✱ FREEZING: Wrap securely in foil or place in freezer bag; seal, label and freeze up to 3 months. Thaw at room temperature.

OATMEAL BREAD

Makes 2 loaves

This whole grain yeast bread is delicious plain or toasted.

2 packages quick-rising active dry yeast
¼ cup sugar
2½ tsps salt
6¼-6½ cups all-purpose flour
2½ cups Quaker Oats (quick or old fashioned, uncooked)
1½ cups water
1¼ cups milk
¼ cup (½ stick) margarine

STEP 6

1. In large mixing bowl, combine yeast, sugar, salt, 3 cups flour and oats; mix well.

2. Heat water, milk and margarine until warm (120°F-130°F).

3. Add to flour mixture. Blend at low speed of electric mixer until moistened; beat 3 minutes at medium speed.

4. By hand, gradually stir in enough remaining flour to make a firm dough.

5. Lightly grease large bowl. Turn dough out onto lightly floured surface. Knead 5-8 minutes or until smooth and elastic.

6. Shape to form balls; place in prepared bowl, turning once to coat surface of dough. Cover; let rise in warm place 30 minutes or until doubled in size.

7. Grease two 8 x 4 or 9 x 5-inch loaf pans.

8. Punch down dough. Cover; let rest 10 minutes.

9. Shape dough to form 2 loaves; place in prepared pans. Brush lightly with additional melted margarine.

10. Cover; let rise in warm place 25 minutes or until doubled in size.

STEP 10

11. Heat oven to 375°F. Bake 45-50 minutes or until dark golden brown. Remove from pans; cool on wire rack before slicing.

Cook's Notes

⌐L⌐ TIME: Preparation takes 30 minutes, rising takes 55 minutes and baking takes about 45 minutes.

◻O◻ SERVING IDEA: This bread will be a welcome change in the lunch box.

BANANA ORANGE MUFFINCAKE
Serves 12

Try this rich, yet delicate muffincake lightly sweetened with ripe bananas and orange juice.

Cake

1½ cups all-purpose flour
1 cup Quaker Oats (quick or old fashioned, uncooked)
⅓ cup firmly packed brown sugar
1 tbsp baking powder
½ tsp baking soda
¼ tsp salt (optional)
⅔ cup mashed, ripe banana (about 2 small)
½ cup orange juice
⅓ cup (5⅓ tbsps) margarine, melted
1 egg, slightly beaten
½ tsp grated orange peel

Glaze

½ cup powdered sugar
1 tbsp orange juice
½ tsp grated orange peel

STEP 4

5. Pour into prepared pan.

6. Bake 30-35 minutes or until golden brown. Cool 10 minutes on wire rack; remove from pan.

7. For glaze, combine ingredients; drizzle evenly over warm cake.

1. Heat oven to 400°F.

2. Grease bottom of 9-inch springform pan or cake pan.

3. For cake, combine first six ingredients; mix well.

4. Add combined banana, juice, margarine, egg and orange peel, mixing just until moistened.

STEP 7

Cook's Notes

⌊ TIME: Preparation takes 10 minutes, cooking takes 30-35 minutes.

? VARIATION: To make muffins, grease 12 medium muffin cups or line with paper baking cups. Prepare batter as recipe directs; fill prepared muffins cups almost full.

Bake 15-18 minutes or until golden brown. Prepare glaze as directed above.

❋ FREEZING: Wrap securely in foil or place in freezer bag; seal, label and freeze up to 3 months.

OLD FASHIONED MEAT LOAF
Serves 8

So easy to prepare – this favorite comfort food will please the whole family.

1½ pounds lean ground beef
¾ cup Quaker Oats (quick or old fashioned, uncooked)
½ cup chopped onion
½ cup tomato sauce or catsup
1 egg, slightly beaten
½ tsp salt (optional)
¼ tsp pepper

1. Heat oven to 350°F.

2. Combine all the ingredients; mix well.

3. Press firmly into 8 x 4-inch loaf pan.

STEP 3

4. Bake 55-60 minutes; drain. Let stand 5 minute before serving.

STEP 2

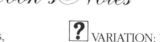

Cook's Notes

TIME: Preparation takes 10 minutes, baking takes 55-60 minutes.

? VARIATION: For meatballs, heat oven to 400°F. Shape meat mixture into 1-inch balls, place on rack in shallow baking pan. Bake 18-20 minutes. Serve meatballs in spaghetti sauce over pasta, if desired. Makes 4 dozen.

ITALIAN STUFFED MEAT LOAF

Serves 6

Surprise your family with this conversation-stopping meat loaf, showcasing the authentic flavors of Italy.

Meat Loaf

1 pound lean ground beef
1 cup Quaker Oats (quick or old fashioned, uncooked)
One 15½-ounce jar spaghetti sauce, divided
½ cup chopped onion
⅓ cup grated Parmesan cheese
1 egg, slightly beaten
1 tbsp Worcestershire sauce
½-1 tsp pepper

Filling

⅓ cup of any one or all of the following: sliced mushrooms, sliced ripe olives, shredded mozzarella cheese, shredded zucchini

Topping

½ cup (2-oz.) shredded mozzarella cheese
Sliced ripe olives

1. Heat oven to 350°F. Grease an 8-inch square baking pan.

2. For meat loaf, combine ground beef, oats, ½ cup spaghetti sauce, onion, Parmesan cheese, egg, Worcestershire sauce and pepper; mix well.

3. Separate mixture into two equal parts. Shape each into a patty about 7-inches in diameter.

4. Place filling on one patty to within ½-inch of edge.

5. Top with other patty.

STEP 4 & 5

6. Pinch sides together to completely enclose filling; smooth edges into rounded loaf.

STEP 6

7. Place into prepared pan. Bake 45-50 minutes or until meat is done.

8. Top loaf with remaining spaghetti sauce and mozzarella cheese. Garnish with olives.

Cook's Notes

t TIME: Preparation takes 25 minutes, cooking takes 45-50 minutes.

SALMON CAKES WITH CUCUMBER SAUCE

Serves 5

This light and colorful cucumber sauce, made with yogurt, is the perfect complement to these golden brown salmon patties.

Sauce
½ cup plain low-fat yogurt
⅓ cup chopped tomato
⅓ cup chopped cucumber
1 tbsp finely chopped onion
1 tbsp snipped fresh dill or 1 tsp dill weed

Salmon Cakes
One 15½-ounce can pink salmon, drained, skin and bones removed
¾ cup Quaker Oats (quick or old fashioned, uncooked)
⅓ cup skim or low-fat milk
1 egg white or whole egg
2 tbsps finely chopped onion
1 tbsp snipped fresh dill or 1 tsp dill weed
¼ tsp salt (optional)
1 tbsp margarine

STEP 2

STEP 3

1. For sauce, combine all ingredients, mix well; chill.

2. For salmon cakes, combine remaining ingredients except margarine; mix well.

3. Shape to form 5 oval patties about 1-inch thick.

4. Pan fry in margarine over medium heat 3-4 minutes on each side or until golden brown and heated through. Serve with sauce.

Cook's Notes

TIME: Preparation takes 20 minutes, cooking takes about 10 minutes.

VARIATION: Substitute two 6½-ounce cans chunk tuna in water, drained and flaked, for salmon.

MEXICALI CHICKEN BREASTS

Serves 4

Make the colorful salsa for this south-of-the-border entree while the chicken is baking.

½ cup Quaker Oats (quick or old fashioned, uncooked)
1 tbsp minced parsley or cilantro
¾ tsp chili powder
¾ tsp paprika
2 whole chicken breasts, split, skinned
3 tbsps margarine, melted
Salsa
2 cups coarsely chopped tomatoes (about 2 medium)
½ cup chopped green pepper
¼ cup coarsely chopped onion
2 tbsps minced parsley or cilantro
1 small clove garlic, minced
1 tbsp lemon juice

---

1. Heat oven to 425°F

2. Place first four ingredients in blender or food processor; cover. Blend about 1 minute, stopping occasionally to stir.

3. Coat chicken with oat mixture.

STEP 3

4. Place on rack in 15 x 10-inch baking pan; gently brush entire surface of chicken with margarine.

5. Bake 35-40 minutes or until juices run clear when pierced with fork.

6. For salsa, combine ingredients; mix well. Serve with chicken.

STEP 2

STEP 6

Cook's Notes

⌐ TIME: Preparation takes 20 minutes, cooking takes 35-40 minutes.

? VARIATION: Add minced, seeded jalapeno pepper or chopped green chilies, drained to salsa for authentic Mexican "heat". Substitute lime juice for lemon juice.

○ SERVING IDEA: Leftover salsa mixture may be covered and refrigerated up to 3 days. Use in tossed salads or serve with grilled fish.

GARDEN-STYLE PIZZA
Serves 8

Try this low-fat, high fiber alternative to regular pizza.

1 cup Quaker Oats (quick or old fashioned, uncooked)
1¼ cups all-purpose flour
1 tsp baking powder
½ tsp salt (optional)
¾ cup skim or low-fat milk
2 tbsps vegetable oil
2 cups sliced mushrooms
1½ cups shredded carrots
1 cup thinly sliced zucchini
½ cup chopped onion
1 tsp vegetable oil
One 8-ounce can pizza sauce
1½ cups (6-oz.) shredded part-skim mozzarella cheese
½ tsp Italian seasoning (optional)

STEP 5

1. Heat oven to 425°F.

2. Spray 12-inch round pizza pan with no stick cooking spray or oil lightly.

3. Place oats in blender container or food processor; cover. Blend about 1 minute, stopping occasionally to stir.

4. Combine ground oats, flour, baking powder and salt. Add milk and oil, stirring with fork until mixture forms a ball. Knead dough on floured surface 10 times.

5. With greased fingers, press dough into prepared pan; shape edge to form rim.

6. Bake 20 minutes or until light golden brown.

7. Sauté mushrooms, carrots, zucchini and onion in oil over medium heat 3 minutes.

8. Spoon pizza sauce evenly over partially baked crust; top with vegetables.

9. Sprinkle with cheese and Italian seasoning; continue to bake 15 minutes or until cheese is melted.

STEP 8

Cook's Notes

⏱ TIME: Preparation takes 20 minutes, cooking takes 30 minutes.

◻ SERVING IDEA: Perfect for a light lunch.

CHICKEN VEGETABLE STIR-FRY

Serves 6

Seasoned chicken strips team up with fresh vegetables for this impressive Oriental dish.

¾ cup Quaker Oats (quick or old fashioned, uncooked)
½ tsp ground ginger
¼ tsp garlic powder
¼ tsp salt (optional)
1¼ pounds skinless, boneless chicken breasts, cut into 1-inch strips
3 tbsps vegetable oil, divided
2 cups broccoli flowerets
1 cup red, green or yellow bell pepper strips
½ cup sliced green onions
1 cup sliced mushrooms
1 tsp chicken flavor instant bouillon granules
1 cup hot water
1 tbsp cornstarch
1 tbsp lite soy sauce

STEP 4

1. Place first four ingredients in blender or food processor; cover. Blend about 1 minute, stopping occasionally to stir; pour mixture into plastic bag.

2. Place chicken pieces in bag; shake until well coated.

3. In large skillet, heat 2 tablespoons oil over medium-high heat.

4. Stir-fry chicken about 6 minutes or until evenly browned and tender. Transfer to serving plate; keep warm.

5. Heat remaining 1 tablespoon oil in skillet; add broccoli, red pepper and green onions; stir-fry 2-3 minutes or until crisp-tender. Add mushrooms; cook 1 minute longer.

STEP 5

6. Dissolve bouillon granules in water. Combine cornstarch and soy sauce, mixing well.

7. Add broth and cornstarch mixture to vegetables. Cook 1-2 minutes or until sauce is thickened and clear. Spoon vegetable mixture over chicken.

Cook's Notes

TIME: Preparation takes 20 minutes, cooking takes 10-15 minutes.

PREPARATION: Purchase pre-cut vegetables from the salad bar at the supermarket to save time in preparation.

SERVING IDEA: Serve over cooked rice or Chinese noodles, if desired.

RAISIN OATMEAL COOKIES

Makes about 4 dozen

An old-fashioned all-time favorite – oatmeal cookies chock-full of raisins.

1 cup (2 sticks) margarine or butter
1¼ cups firmly packed brown sugar
2 eggs
½ tsp vanilla
1¼ cups all-purpose flour
1 tsp baking soda
½ tsp salt (optional)
½ tsp ground cinnamon
3 cups Quaker Oats (quick or old fashioned, uncooked)
1 cup raisins
1 cup chopped nuts (optional)

1. Heat oven to 350°F.

2. Beat margarine and sugar until fluffy, add eggs and vanilla, mixing well.

STEP 2

3. Add combined flour, soda, salt and cinnamon, mixing well.

4. Stir in oats, raisins and nuts.

STEP 4

5. Drop by rounded tablespoonfuls onto greased cookie sheet.

STEP 5

6. Bake 10-12 minutes or until light golden brown.

7. Cool 1 minute on cookie sheet; remove to wire rack. Cool completely. Store tightly covered.

Cook's Notes

🕐 TIME: Preparation takes 15 minutes, baking takes about 40 minutes.

❓ VARIATION: Substitute semi-sweet chocolate, butterscotch or peanut butter pieces for raisins.

✳ FREEZING: Wrap securely in foil or place in freezer bag; seal, label and freeze up to 3 months. Thaw at room temperature.

SNOW COVERED ALMOND CRESCENTS

Makes about 4 dozen

Dusted with powdered sugar, these cookies have a festive, holiday appearance.

1 cup (2 sticks) margarine or butter, softened
¾ cup powdered sugar
½ tsp almond extract or 2 tsps vanilla
2 cups all-purpose flour
¼ tsp salt (optional)
1 cup Quaker Oats (quick or old fashioned, uncooked)
½ cup finely chopped almonds
Powdered sugar

1. Heat oven to 325°F.

2. Beat margarine, sugar and almond extract until fluffy. Add flour and salt; mix until well blended. Stir in oats and almonds.

STEP 2

3. Using level measuring tablespoonfuls, shape dough into crescents.

STEP 3

4. Bake on ungreased cookie sheet 14-17 minutes or until bottoms are light golden brown. Remove to wire rack.

5. Sift additional powdered sugar generously over warm cookies.

STEP 5

6. Cool completely. Store tightly covered.

Cook's Notes

🕐 TIME: Preparation takes 10 minutes, baking takes about 1 hour.

✳ FREEZING: Wrap securely in foil or place in freezer bag; seal, label and freeze up to 3 months. Thaw at room temperature.

JUMBO OAT COOKIES

Makes 1 dozen

A healthy low-fat cookie with a hint of almond.

¾ cup sugar
⅓ cup (5⅓ tbsps) margarine, softened
⅓ cup light corn syrup
2 egg whites, slightly beaten
1 tsp almond extract
2¼ cups Quaker Oats (quick or old fashioned, uncooked)
1 cup all-purpose flour
½ tsp baking soda
½ tsp salt (optional)
3 tbsps sliced almonds

1. Heat oven to 350°F.

2. Beat sugar, margarine and corn syrup until fluffy.

STEP 2

3. Add egg whites and almond extract; mix well.

4. Gradually add combined remaining ingredients; mix well.

5. Drop by ¼ cup measure about 2-inches apart onto ungreased cookie sheet.

STEP 5

6. Press with fingertips into 3-inch circles.

STEP 6

7. Bake 14-16 minutes or until light golden brown.

8. Cool 1 minute on cookie sheet. Remove to aluminum foil; cool completely.

Cook's Notes

⏱ TIME: Preparation takes 15 minutes, baking takes about 30 minutes.

❄ FREEZING: Wrap securely in foil or place in freezer bag; seal, label and freeze up to 3 months. Thaw at room temperature.

CHEWY BLOND BROWNIES
Makes 2 dozen

For a decadent dessert, top with vanilla ice cream and hot fudge sauce.

⅔ cup (11 tbsps) margarine or butter, softened
1¼ cups firmly packed brown sugar
1⅓ cups Quaker Oats (quick or old fashioned, uncooked)
1⅓ cup all-purpose flour
2 eggs
½ cup semi-sweet chocolate pieces
½ cup chopped nuts
2 tsps vanilla
½ tsp salt (optional)
¾ tsp baking soda

1. Heat oven to 350°F. Grease a 13 x 9-inch baking pan.

2. In large bowl, beat margarine and sugar until well blended.

STEP 2

3. Add remaining ingredients; mix well.

STEP 3

4. Spread into prepared pan.

STEP 4

5. Bake 25-30 minutes or until golden brown.

6. Cool; cut into squares.

Cook's Notes

 TIME: Preparation takes 20 minutes, baking takes 25-30 minutes.

? VARIATION: For iced brownies, sprinkle one 12-ounce package (2 cups) chocolate pieces over brownies immediately after baking. Let stand 10 minutes; spread melted chocolate evenly with spatula. Cool completely before cutting.

✱ FREEZING: Wrap securely in foil or place in freezer bag; seal, label and freeze up to 3 months. Thaw at room temperature.

I LOVE YOU SHORTCAKES

Makes 6 shortcakes

Perfect for Valentine's day and pretty enough for any special occasion.

Shortcakes

1½ cups all-purpose flour
½ cup Quaker Oats (quick or old fashioned, uncooked)
2 tbsps sugar
1 tbsp baking powder
¼ tsp salt (optional)
½ cup (1 stick) margarine
½ cup skim or low-fat milk

Topping for 2 servings

1 tbsp water
1 tbsp sugar
1 tsp lemon juice
½ cup fresh or frozen peeled, sliced peaches, thawed
½ cup fresh or frozen red raspberries or other berries, thawed

STEP 3

STEP 5

1. Heat oven to 425°F.

2. For shortcakes, combine flour, oats, sugar, baking powder and salt.

3. Cut in margarine until mixture resembles coarse crumbs. Add milk, mix just until dry ingredients are moistened.

4. Shape dough to form a ball; knead gently on lightly floured surface 10 times.

5. Pat dough to ½-inch thickness; cut with 3-inch heart shaped or round biscuit cutter. Place on ungreased cookie sheet.

6. Bake 12-14 minutes or until golden brown.

7. For topping combine the water, sugar and lemon juice in small saucepan. Cook over medium heat, stirring until sugar is dissolved.

8. Add peaches and raspberries; cook 1-2 minutes or until fruit is heated through.

9. Split 2 shortcakes. Place on individual dessert plates. Spoon fruit mixture over shortcakes; top with low-fat vanilla yogurt, if desired.

Cook's Notes

TIME: Preparation takes 10 minutes, baking takes 12-14 minutes.

PREPARATION: Using a pastry blender makes fast work of cutting in margarine.

VARIATION: For toppings, serve with thawed raspberries or strawberries in lite syrup for a quick topping. Shortcakes make great biscuits!

SERVING IDEA: In season, serve with fresh berries and whipped cream.

FREEZING: Wrap securely in foil or place in freezer bag; seal, label and freeze up to 3 months. Thaw at room temperature.

BLUEBERRY OAT BARS

Makes 15 bars

Bring these rich and delicious bars to your next family gathering.

Crust

1¾ cups Quaker Oats (quick or old fashioned, uncooked)
1½ cups all-purpose flour
¾ cup firmly packed brown sugar
½ cup chopped nuts
½ tsp baking soda
¼ tsp salt (optional)
¾ cup (1½ sticks) margarine or butter, melted

Filling

2 cups fresh or frozen blueberries
½ cup sugar
3 tbsps water
2 tbsps cornstarch
1 tbsp lemon juice

1. Heat oven to 350°F. Grease 11 x 7-inch glass baking dish.

2. Combine dry ingredients for crust. Add margarine, mixing until crumbly.

3. Reserve 1 cup; press remaining mixture onto bottom of prepared dish. Bake 10 minutes.

4. In small saucepan, combine blueberries, sugar and 2 tablespoons water.

5. Bring to a boil and simmer uncovered for 2 minutes, stirring occasionally.

6. Combine cornstarch, remaining 1 tablespoon water and lemon juice; mix well.

STEP 3

7. Gradually stir into blueberry mixture; cook and stir about 30 seconds or until thickened.

8. Spread filling over partially baked base to within ¼-inch of dish; sprinkle with reserved oat mixture.

STEP 8

9. Bake 18-20 minutes or until topping is golden brown. Cool, and cut into bars. Store tightly covered.

Cook's Notes

🕐 TIME: Preparation takes 15 minutes, baking takes about 18-20 minutes.

◯ SERVING IDEA: Give your kids these delicious bars as an after-school snack.

DOUBLE CHOCOLATE OAT COOKIES

Makes about 3 dozen

Rich and delicious, these double chocolate cookies are sure to please the whole family.

One 12-ounce package semi-sweet chocolate
   pieces, divided (about 2 cups)
½ cup margarine or butter, softened
½ cup sugar
1 egg
¼ tsp vanilla
¾ cup all-purpose flour
¾ cup Quaker Oats (quick or old fashioned,
   uncooked)
1 tsp baking powder
¼ tsp salt (optional)
¼ tsp baking soda

1. Heat oven to 375°F.

2. Melt 1 cup chocolate pieces in small saucepan;
set aside.

STEP 2

3. Beat margarine and sugar until fluffy; add
melted chocolate, egg and vanilla.

STEP 3

4. Add combined flour, oats, baking powder, salt
and baking soda; mix well.

5. Stir in remaining chocolate pieces.

6. Drop by rounded tablespoonfuls onto
ungreased cookie sheet.

STEP 6

7. Bake 8-10 minutes. Cool 1 minute on cookie
sheet; remove to wire rack.

Cook's Notes

⏱ TIME: Preparation takes 15 minutes,
baking takes about 30 minutes in total.

✳ FREEZING: Wrap securely in foil or place
in freezer bag; seal, label and freeze up to 3
months. Thaw at room temperature.

KISS O' LEMON POUND CAKE

Serves 16

Serve this rich, delicate cake by the slice with tangy raspberry sauce as the grand finale to any meal.

1 cup Quaker Oats (quick or old fashioned,
    uncooked)
1¾ cups all-purpose flour
1 tsp baking powder
½ tsp salt (optional)
1¼ cups sugar
1 cup (2 sticks) margarine or butter, softened
3 eggs
2 tbsps grated lemon peel (about 3 lemons)
¾ cup milk
Powdered sugar
One 10-ounce package frozen red raspberries,
    thawed

STEP 5

1. Heat oven to 350°F. Grease and flour 9 x 5-inch loaf pan.

2. Place oats in blender container or food processor; cover. Blend about 1 minute, stopping occasionally to stir.

3. Combine oats with flour, baking powder and salt. Set aside.

4. Beat sugar and margarine until fluffy. Add eggs and lemon peel; mix well.

5. Add combined dry ingredients alternately with milk, mixing until well blended.

6. Pour into prepared pan. Bake 1 hour 10 minutes or until toothpick inserted in center comes out clean.

7. Cool 10 minutes in pan. Remove to wire rack; cool completely. Sprinkle with powdered sugar.

8. In blender or food processor, blend raspberries until smooth. Serve sauce with pound cake.

STEP 8

Cook's Notes

⏱ TIME: Preparation takes 20 minutes, baking takes 1 hour 10 minutes.

❓ VARIATION: Substitute your favorite berries for raspberries.

FRESH FRUIT CRISP

Serves 9

Your favorite fruit, layered beneath a crunchy oat topping makes a wholesome, old-fashioned dessert.

Topping

1 cup Quaker Oats (quick or old fashioned, uncooked)
¼ cup firmly packed brown sugar
¼ cup (½ stick) margarine, melted
¼ tsp ground cinnamon

Filling

¼ cup firmly packed brown sugar
¼ cup water
2 tbsps all-purpose flour
½ tsp ground cinnamon
6 cups peeled, sliced peaches, pears or apples (6-8 medium)

1. Heat oven to 350°F.

2. For topping, combine ingredients, mix well; set aside.

STEP 2

3. For filling, combine dry ingredients, mixing well. Add fruit, tossing to coat.

STEP 3

4. Spoon into 8-inch square glass baking dish.

5. Top with reserved oat mixture.

STEP 5

6. Bake 40-45 minutes or until fruit is tender.

Microwave Directions: Prepare as directed in steps 1-4 above. Microwave at HIGH 6 minutes, stirring once. Top with reserved oat mixture. Microwave at HIGH for 3-6 minutes or until fruit is tender.

Cook's Notes

⏱ TIME: Preparation takes 15 minutes, baking takes 40-45 minutes.

◎ SERVING IDEA: Serve warm with vanilla yogurt or ice milk.

BLACK FOREST CHEESECAKE
Serves 16

This Bavarian-style cheesecake is perfect for entertaining.

Crust
1½ cups Quaker Oats (quick or old fashioned, uncooked)
½ cup finely chopped nuts
⅓ cup firmly packed brown sugar
⅓ cup (5⅓ tbsps) margarine or butter, melted

Filling
Two 8-ounce packages cream cheese, softened
⅔ cup sugar
1 tsp vanilla
2 eggs
1 cup (6-oz.) semi-sweet chocolate pieces, melted
¼ cup whipping cream

Topping
One 21-ounce can cherry pie filling

STEP 3

6. Beat in chocolate and cream until well blended.

7. Pour into cooled crust. Bake 1 hour or until center is almost set.

8. Cool completely before removing rim. Chill 6 hours or overnight.

9. To serve, spread pie filling over top.

1. Heat oven to 350°F. Grease bottom and sides of 9-inch springform pan.

2. For crust, combine ingredients; mix well.

3. Press firmly onto bottom and 1-inch up from sides of prepared pan. Bake 15 minutes. Cool completely.

4. For filling, beat cream cheese, sugar and vanilla at medium speed of electric mixer until fluffy.

5. Add eggs, one at a time, beating well after each addition.

STEP 9

Cook's Notes

⌐ TIME: Preparation takes 30 minutes, baking takes about 1 hour, and chilling takes 6 hours.

◣ PREPARATION: If seal on springform pan is not tight, wrap piece of aluminum foil over bottom of pan to avoid leakage. Cool completely before refrigerating to avoid moisture condensation.

❓ VARIATION: For Rich Chocolate Cheesecake, omit cherry topping.

○ SERVING IDEA: Garnish with whipped cream, grated chocolate or chocolate curls, if desired.

PEAR N' CRANBERRY COBBLER

Serves 8

Dazzle your family with this festive fresh pear and tangy cranberry cobbler.

Filling
½ cup light corn syrup
⅓ cup sugar
1 tbsp cornstarch
1½ cups fresh or frozen cranberries
2 medium pears, unpeeled, sliced

Topping
¾ cup all-purpose flour
½ cup sugar
⅓ cup (5⅓ tbsps) margarine or butter
1 cup Quaker Oats (quick or old fashioned, uncooked)
1 egg, slightly beaten

1. Heat oven to 400°F. Grease a 9-inch square or round baking pan.

2. For filling, in medium saucepan, combine corn syrup, sugar and cornstarch, mixing well. Stir in cranberries.

STEP 2

3. Heat to a boil; reduce heat. Simmer 5 minutes, or until cranberries pop open.

4. Stir in pears. Pour into prepared pan.

STEP 4

5. For topping, combine flour and sugar. Cut in margarine until mixture resembles coarse crumbs.

6. Stir in oats; mix well. Add egg, mixing until moistened. Crumble evenly over fruit.

STEP 6

7. Bake 30-35 minutes or until top is golden brown.

Cook's Notes

⏱ TIME: Preparation takes 20 minutes, baking takes 30-35 minutes.

◯ SERVING IDEA: Great served hot with whipped cream or vanilla ice cream.

ORANGE PUMPKIN TART

Serves 12

This delightful tart is reminiscent of traditional pumpkin pie. The orange drizzle adds just the right touch to this healthy holiday favorite.

1½ cups all-purpose flour
1 cup Quaker Oats (quick or old fashioned, uncooked), divided
1 cup plus 2 tbsps sugar, divided
¾ cup (1½ sticks) margarine
2 tbsps water
One 16-ounce can (1¾ cups) pumpkin
1 egg white
1 tsp pumpkin pie spice
½ cup powdered sugar
2 tsps orange juice
½ tsp grated orange peel

---

1. Heat oven to 400°F.

2. Combine flour, ¾ cup oats and ½ cup sugar; cut in margarine until crumbly. Reserve ¾ cup mixture.

3. Mix remaining mixture and water until moistened.

STEP 4

4. Divide into two parts; press each onto cookie sheet to form two 12 x 5-inch tarts.

5. Combine pumpkin, ½ cup sugar, egg white and spice. Spread over tarts.

STEP 5

6. Top with combined ¼ cup oats, 2 tablespoons sugar and reserved oat mixture.

STEP 6

7. Bake 25 to 28 minutes or until golden brown; cool.

8. Drizzle with combined remaining ingredients.

Cook's Notes

TIME: Preparation takes 30 minutes, baking takes 25-28 minutes.

COOK'S TIP: Refrigerate all leftovers.

? VARIATION: Substitute sweet potato for pumpkin.

INDEX

Recipes developed by The Quaker Kitchens
Photography by Peter Barry
Recipes styled by Helen Burdett
Designed by Judith Chant
Project co-ordination by Hanni Penrose